# Tractors, Diggers & Dozers

# A Picture Book For Kids

## A Childhood Education Science Book About Tractors, Diggers & Bulldozers

By Lilley Light

ISBN: 10: 149215119X
ISBN-13: 978-1492151197

# DEDICATION

This book is dedicated to my 2 year old (and a bit) grandson 'Sean Bailey' who's love of heavy machinery knows no bounds and is the inspiration for this book.

**Tractors, Diggers & Dozers**
A Picture Book For Kids

# CONTENTS

# AUTHOR'S STATEMENT

The information presented in this book has been researched and checked for accuracy. However, the author and publishers make no warranty, express or implied, that the information contained herein is appropriate for every individual, situation, or purpose and assume no responsibility for errors, or omissions. The reader assumes full risk and responsibility for all actions taken as a result of the information contained within this book and the author will not be held responsible for any loss or damage, whether consequential, incidental, or otherwise that may result from the information presented in this book.

This book is just a small snapshot of the information that is available for Tractors, Diggers and Dozers and is intended to provide a visual introduction to these machines.

I have relied on my own experiences as well as many different sources for the information contained within this book and have done my best to ensure the facts are correct and to give credit where it is due. In the event that any material is incorrect, or has been used without proper permission, please contact me so that the oversight can be rectified.

*I do hope you enjoy reading it as much as I have enjoyed writing it,*

*Lilley Light.*

.

# INTRODUCTION

Tractors, Diggers and Dozers are fascinating, especially for youngsters who are eager to learn about such things.

I know that my young grandson just loves seeing these large machines in action and his Mom takes him to the local shipyard so that he can watch big trucks being loaded with long tree trunks by diggers fitted with special claws.

# HEAVY MACHINERY

Heavy Machinery includes all those vehicles that help us build, move, mine, dig and transport heavy things and are used on farms, roads and for building and mining.

*Can you name all of the vehicles in this picture?*

| | |
|---|---|
| Cement Mixer | Digger |
| Dozer or Bulldozer | Dump Truck |
| Roller | Excavator |

*Answers to Questions*

# TRACTORS

*Old Tractor used by a greengrocer*

Tractors are a means of transport, most often for a farm worker. Tractors produce high power at very low speed. They are used to haul machinery or a trailer in farming industries or construction work. Originally tractors were used just for land preparation, but nowadays they do a lot more. In addition, farm or construction tools can either be fixed to the tractor or they can be towed behind it.

*Tractor used to pull a trailer for farming purposes*

Tractors are strong and sturdy which makes them ideal for lots of different tasks. Dozer blades, hoes, buckets, rippers and other accessories can be fitted to a tractor. The main addition to the front of a tractor are buckets or dozer blades. When these tools are attached to a tractor the tractor is called a Bulldozer (Dozer for short) or an Excavator.

*Tractor with Dozer blade fitted*

Farm tools were first developed in the early 19th century. Using a flexible belt, steam engines were connected to all sorts of farm machinery.

*Steam Sawmill Tractor*

These steam engines were then used to power large tractors called Traction Engines, which were used to pull wagons or plows.

*Steam Traction Engine*

Steam-powered engines remained in use until reliable petrol engines had been developed. In 1892 at Iowa, USA, John Froelich is credited with inventing and constructing the first tractor powered by a gasoline/petrol engine.

*1947 Garden Tractor*

The first affordable tractor that was mass-produced was the Fordson Model F produced by Henry Ford, the famous car maker. It was built in 1916 and made it possible for farmers to buy a tractor for the first time. In 1917 the Fordson tractor was made available to the public in October 1917 for the princely sum of $750.

*A 1936 Fordson Model N Tractor (photo care of Wikimedia Commons)*

The word 'Tractor' is commonly used for a variety of vehicles. The farm tractor is mainly used to prepare land for the raising of crops using a variety of attachments that are towed by the tractor.

*Early Farm Tractor*

The standard farm tractor is open to the elements and has two big driving wheels on the rear with two small front wheels. It has a single seat and the large engine is located in front of the driver. Nowadays some tractors have enclosed cabs with heating and cooling to improve the working conditions for the driver, who can spend many hours sitting in the 'saddle' of their tractor.

*Modern Tractor working in a Tulip field*

Farm Tractors have been made for special uses such as 'row crop' Tractors, so that they can travel down rows of crops like corn, tomatoes, vines, or other crops without damaging the plants. These Tractors are built to suit the growing of crops in rows.

*Row Crop Tractor in operation*

Tractors can be used to grade roads, move logs from one place to another, excavate and landscape. Different types of attachments can be fitted to a tractor, including backhoes, pallet forks, front loaders, etc.

*Log Yard Tractor*

Small Tractors are used for gardens or cutting lawns and they are designed for garden and landscape maintenance. Garden tractors are used for cutting grass, snow removal, and small land maintenance. Common implements for these small tractors include a box blade, a grader blade, a landscape rake, a post hole digger, rotary cutter or slasher, a mid, or rear-mount mower, a seeder and a rotary tiller.

*Lawn Tractor with snow plough fitted*

Aircraft tractors, also called 'Tugs', are used in airports to move aircraft on the ground, usually to push aircraft away, or tow them from, their parking stands.

*Tug ready to move an aircraft from its parking stand*

The latest use for tractors is to move rocket ships and other space bound craft from wherever they are located to their launch areas.

*Rocket being readied for take-off by a large tractor*
*– image attributed to NASA*

These enormous bulldozers move very slowly, about one mile in an hour when they are transporting a rocket ship and a team of up to 11 people is required to control and monitor the slow progress.

# BACKHOE LOADER

A Backhoe Loader, or simply 'hoe' is probably the main change to a standard tractor. It has a backhoe on the back of the tractor to lift dirt, rubble or other material and a loader on the front of it to lift and dump material into a waiting truck.

Backhoe Loaders are very common and can be used for a wide variety of tasks such as demolition work, construction, moving building materials from one place to another, digging holes, loading trucks, paving roads, breaking up roads, etc.

The ability for precise control of the front bucket, combined with their compact size and versatility, make Backhoe Loaders a very useful tool for urban maintenance projects, including repairs and construction in confined spaces.

*Typical Backhoe Loader*

# BULLDOZER OR DOZER

A Dozer is really a powerful Tractor fitted with continuous tracks, instead of wheels for extra grip and they have a large blade on the front to push or drag material.

Bulldozers were first designed by a farmer 'James Cummings' and a draftsman 'J. Earl McLeod' in 1923 and their design was based on a farm tractor used for plowing fields.

*Early Bulldozer clearing forest litter*

Bulldozers have changed over time to become machines that are capable of working in ways that the original bulldozer couldn't. For example, by replacing the blade for a big bucket they can be used to scoop up earth, rocks or other loose material to load into waiting trucks.

*Bulldozer with a large bucket working in a quarry*

Other changes to the original Bulldozer design include making it smaller so that it can operate where space is limited. By making them very small they can be used in tiny areas such as people's back yards, these small Dozers are better known as a 'Bobcat' after the original manufacturer.

*Small Excavator 'Bobcat' in action*

During World War 1 (1914 to 1918) armored bulldozers were used to clear the path for troops and equipment following behind. They were also used for earth moving, setting off bombs, clearing obstacles, opening up routes and demolishing buildings. The heavy armor plating fitted to the bulldozers protected the operator from enemy fire.

*Heavy-duty Soviet military Dozer in action*

# DIGGERS

Diggers are really Excavators with as shovel and are used to dig trenches, holes or foundations and usually have tracks instead of wheels like Dozers for a better grip on the ground.

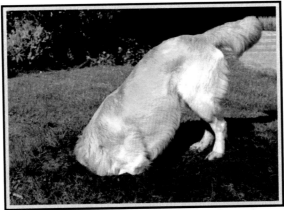

*Oops, wrong sort of digger, how about this one?*

*Digger / Excavator working on a hillside*

# EXCAVATORS

Excavators consist of a boom and a stick with a bucket on the end. They have a cab for the driver that sits on a moving platform. The driver's cab is located on top of the chassis which has either tracks or wheels attached.

*Excavator Loader with raised Backhoe*

Excavators are also called mechanical shovels, backhoes, or 360-degree excavators (sometimes abbreviated to '360') they are very versatile and are used for:
- Digging trenches, holes, foundations
- Moving rocks, stones, or other material
- Forestry work
- Demolition
- General grading or landscaping
- Lifting or moving heavy weights like large pipes, or concrete slabs
- Mining, usually open-pit mining
- Driving piles into the ground when used with a Pile Driver.

There are many other attachments that can be used with an Excavator such as borers, rippers, crushers, cutters, lifters and other attachments. Excavators are usually employed together with Bulldozers and trucks when working on a large site.

*Excavator demolishing an old house*

# A MESSAGE FROM THE AUTHOR

I do hope that you have enjoyed reading and looking at the pictures in this book about *Tractors, Diggers and Dozers.*

If you did enjoy it, please consider leaving an Amazon book review by going to Amazon.com and entering 'B00EEJRZC4' in the Search box to locate my Kindle book and enter your thoughts as it is the best way to let other people know about this fun, fact filled book, I would really appreciate it.

Many thanks, *Lilley Light*

*These kids are enjoying playing on an old Tractor!*

Made in the USA
Lexington, KY
18 November 2018